© The Association of Cost Engineers
33 Ovington Square, London SW3 1LJ, and
The Royal Institution of Chartered Surveyors
12 Great George Street, Parliament Square, Londn SW1P 3AD

December 1984

First Edition

ISBN: 0 9510094 1 9

Printed in Great Britain by **The Jupiter Press Limited, Croydon, Surrey**

STANDARD METHOD OF MEASUREMENT
For
Industrial Engineering Construction

Authorised by Agreement between
The Association of Cost Engineers and
The Royal Institution of Chartered Surveyors

THE JOINT DOCUMENTATION BOARD
The Association of Cost Engineers
33 Ovington Square
London SW3 1LJ

&

The Royal Institution of Chartered Surveyors
12 Great George Street
Parliament Square
London SW1P 3AD

Foreword

There has been a need for a comprehensive standard method of measurement for industrial engineering construction (SMMIEC) for some years. The need was first recognised by the Institute of Quantity Surveyors resulting in the Formation in 1980 of the Joint Documentation Board (JDB) comprising members in equal numbers of the Association of Cost Engineers, the Institute of Quantity Surveyors and The Royal Institution of Chartered Surveyors.

The JDB under the Chairmanship of Michael Millwood, FRICS, FCIOB, ACIArb has produced the first edition which is set forth in the following pages. During the progress of the work the Institute of Quantity Surveyors unified with The Royal Institution of Chartered Suurveyors and it was in keeping with the spirit of co-operation which exists between the two remaining constituent bodies, that arrangements were made for those members of the former Institute of Quantity Surveyors to continue to make their valuable contribution as members of the JDB.

The Joint Documentation Board is comprised as follows:—

Representing the Association of Cost Engineers

    D P M Harris, MACostE, F.Inst.Pet
    A E Jackson, FRICS, MACostE
    P L Marsh, ARICS, MACostE
    D F Parkinson, FRICS, MACostE
    V Thompson, MACostE
    R B Watson, FRICS, MACostE

Representing the Royal Institution of Chartered Surveyors

    J H Blenkhorn, ARICS, MACostE, F.Inst.Pet
    R P Davison, BA, FRICS, MACostE, ACIArb
    R T Marshall, FRICS, FCIArb, MACostE
    W E Povall, FRICS, MACostE
    I R Sisley, FRICS, MACostE
    M J Wade, FRICS, MACostE

The members of the Working Party responsible to the JDB for preparing the SMMIEC were:—

    D F Parkinson, FRICS, MACostE, (Chairman)
    J H Blenkhorn, ARICS, MACostE, F.Inst.Pet
    P Cummins, ARICS, MCIOB
    A E Jackson, FRICS, MACostE
    P L Marsh, ARICS, MACostE
    I R Sisley, FRICS, MACostE
    V Thompson, MACostE
    M J Wade, FRICS, MACostE
    B G Wheeler, FRICS, MACostE
    J Wilson, FRICS, MACostE

We should like to express our thanks on behalf of Councils of the two Sponsoring Bodies to all of those members who have contributed so much of their time and effort in the production of this First Edition.

President (Brian Wheeler)
The Association of Cost Engineers

President of Quantity Surveyors Division (Peter Graham)
The Royal Institution of Chartered Surveyors

DECEMBER 1984

DECEMBER 1984

Contents

Preface to the First Edition

Purpose

The purpose of the S.M.M.I.E.C. is to contribute to the framework of project documentation, and in particular to provide measurement principles for the estimating, tendering, contract management and cost control aspects of industrial engineering construction.

The term Industrial Engineering Construction shall mean equipment, facilities and structures which will ultimately carry out a mechanical function, a manufacturing activity or a process operation, and the S.M.M.I.E.C. is particularly aimed at projects emanating from the following industries:—

        (a)   Chemical.
        (b)   Petroleum.
        (c)   Nuclear.
        (d)   Gas Exploration and Production.
        (e)   Oil Exploration and Production.
        (f)   Power Generation.
        (g)   Food and Drink.
        (h)   Refining.
        (i)   Steel Production.
        (j)   Pharmaceuticals.

Use of Other Methods

A particular feature of the S.M.M.I.E.C. is the recognition of the need to separate fabrication from erection, and the common practice of supplying materials and equipment as "Free Issue" to the Contractor.

This S.M.M.I.E.C. does not seek to clash with recognised Methods of Measurement applicable to other areas of the construction industry, and this has inevitably lead to a restriction in the number of work sections covered.

The use of Standard Methods of Measurement for Civil Engineering, Building Work and Pipelines will not be affected. Reference to these methods will continue to be necessary when measuring civil engineering construction, building work, architectural fit-out or finishes, and cross-country pipelines.

Where it is necessary to depart from the Method of Measurement or where an alternative method of measurement is used this shall be clearly stated.

Joint Steering Committee

A Joint Steering Committee will monitor, review and maintain the S.M.M.I.E.C. for the benefit of all users.

Consultation

In producing the S.M.M.I.E.C. particular attention was directed towards consultation with trade association, contractors, client organisations and professional bodies.

A list of those who responded to the consultative documents is given at the end and the Sponsoring Bodies are most grateful for their help and advice. Additionally, appreciation is extended to all those Members, Consultancies and Regional Committees of the Sponsoring Bodies who so ably contributed technical advice and practice guidance during the consultative stage.

Section A
GENERAL RULES

A.1 SCOPE OF METHOD OF MEASUREMENT

The scope of this document embraces the rules for the measurement of industrial engineering construction work.

A.2 DEFINITIONS

In the Method of Measurement the following words and expressions shall be interpreted in the manner shown, except where expressly indicated otherwise:

1. Works means the whole of the work to be executed in accordance with the Contract.
2. Provisional Sum means a sum provided for work or for costs which cannot be entirely foreseen, defined or detailed at the time of Tender and which shall be the subject of a subsequent instruction once requirements are established.
3. Prime Cost Sum means a sum provided for work or services to be executed by a Nominated Sub-Contractor, or for materials or goods to be obtained from a Nominated Supplier. Such a sum shall be deemed to be exclusive of any Contractor's profit or attendances as Clauses A.8 and A.9 hereafter.
4. Supply shall be deemed to include the procurement or provision from stock to specified requirements, expediting, inspecting, packing and protecting, haulage, storage, delivery to place of fabrication or erection and for all directly associated costs.
5. Fabricate, or Fabrication, shall be deemed to include taking delivery, off-loading, checking, sorting and the acceptance of materials and components into Fabricator's control, the preparation of any neceassry fabrication sketches and calculations, temporary/trial fit up, alignment, packaging of the finished fabrications, storing, loading and haulage to place of erection or other specified location.
6. Erect, Erection, Install, Installation or Fixing of materials, fabrications, assemblies, spools, components, plant, equipment and the like shall each be deemed to include taking delivery, off-loading, checking, sorting, storing, loading and haulage to place of erection, hoisting, provision and use of temporary supports and bracings, temporary/trial erection, fixing and securing into final position.
7. Datum shall mean the nominated prime surface of the ground or structure identified on the drawings.
8. Free Issue Materials are items supplied to the Contractor, purchased by others for incorporation into the Works.
9. Extra Over where used within this document shall mean the additional requirements in provision of labour, plant, materials and consumables in performing the specific operation referred to.

A.3 THE SITE AND WORKS

1. Working heights or depths shall be stated relative to datum.
2. Alteration work or work in or to existing structures or installations shall each be given under separate headings stating the location of the work and the ownership of any existing materials to be removed. The operational condition of the plant at the time of the work shall be stated, together with a description of any chemical hazard or contamination likely to be encountered. Treatment or transfer to special disposal areas shall be detailed.
3. All work required to be carried out in hazardous conditions, with the use of hazard-proof plant or otherwise to comply with special requirements shall be given separately. Work to be carried out in or under water shall be so described, stating whether canal, river or sea water and, where applicable, the mean spring tide levels of high and low water.
4. Where restrictions are encountered requiring Work Permit authorisation, this shall be stated and a copy of the Procedures included with the Tender documentation.
5. Where the Works are required to be caried out off site at a Fabricator's Yard or other facility, this shall be stated, complete with delivery or load-out requirements.
6. Where dismantling and/or re-fixing is specifically required, this shall be described under a separate heading.

A.4 DESIGN INFORMATION

1. General arrangement drawings, piping and instrument diagrams, foundation, structure and underground service drawings, schedules and other relevant design information indicating the scope, location and type of work to be carried out shall, where available, accompany the quantities or schedules.
2. Where the Contractor is required to carry out any engineering design and drawing work this shall be stated. The extent of the work and responsibility for the same shall be defined.
3. In the absence of adequate Specification information, descriptions on the drawings or within Bills of Quantities, Schedules of Rates and the like shall be amplified to comply with the requirements of this document.

A.5 METHOD OF MEASUREMENT

1. The units of measurement shall be:
   - (a) Metre.
   - (b) Number.
   - (c) Kilogram.
   - (d) Tonne.
2. Work shall be measured net as fixed in position and each measurement shall be taken to the nearest 10mm. Measurements of less than 5mm shall be disregarded and measurements of 5mm and over shall be regarded as 10mm. This rule shall not apply to any dimensions stated in the descriptions.
3. Quantities shall be totalled to the nearest whole unit. Fractions of a unit less than a half shall be disregarded and all other fractions shall be regarded as whole units. Where the application of this Clause would cause an entire item to be eliminated then such item shall be enumerated, stating the size or weight as appropriate, or alternatively taken as one whole unit.
4. The order of stating the dimensions in descriptions shall be in the sequence of length, width and height. Where ambiguity could arise the dimensions shall be specifically identified.
5. Unless specifically required herein, temporary work shall not be measured but shall be deemed to be included within the item to which it applies.
6. Nominal size or diameter where referred to in relation to pipework measurement, shall, as A.P.I. (American Petroleum Institute) Specification, mean internal diameter (I.D.) on pipework up to and including 12in. and external diameter (O.D.) on pipework exceeding 12in., and this shall apply throughout unless otherwise stated.
7. Notwithstanding the provisions in this Method of Measurement for items and operations to be measured and detailed individually, they may, only where circumstances do not permit otherwise, be given in an all-inclusive description, provided attention is drawn to the work coverage of the all-inclusive item in each and every case.

A.6 FREE ISSUE MATERIALS

Where materials are to be supplied as free issue, this shall be stated together with details of:
1. Point of delivery or collection and responsibility for handling, together with a schedule of delivery key dates.
2. Material test certificates and indentification.
3. Methods of protection, storage and associated preparatory work such as degreasing and cleaning.
4. Condition of steelwork and pipework ends.
5. Responsibility for reconciliation and storage of material whilst in the care of the Contractor and return of surplus and scrap.

A.7 DESCRIPTIONS

The following shall be deemed to be included in an item unless otherwise stated:
1. Labour and all costs in connection therewith.
2. Use of construction plant and tools.
3. Materials and all costs in connection therewith.
4. Allowance for waste.
5. Consumable stores, including jointing materials (but excluding gaskets and bolts, nuts and washers), welding rods, water and power, fuel and the like and all costs in connection therewith.
6. Test certificates, mill certificates, identification and general inspection requirements.
7. Welder qualification testing and welding procedure approval. The responsibility for the supply of testing materials shall be stated.
8. Establishment and overhead charges, except where provided under Section B, and profit.
9. Temporary works, except where provided under Section C.
10. Templates.
11. Return of empty containers.
12. Clearing away rubbish.

A.8 PROFIT ON PRIME COST SUMS

Prime Cost Sums shall be exclusive of any profit or costs required by the Contractor and an item shall be given after each such sum for the addition thereof.

A.9 ATTENDANCES

1. General attendance on Nominated Sub-Contractors shall be given as an item in each case and shall, unless stated otherwise, be deemed to include only:

   - (a) Allowing use of standing scaffolding, mess-rooms, sanitary accommodation and welfare facilities.
   - (b) Providing space for office accommodation and for storage of plant and materials.
   - (c) Providing light and water.
   - (d) Clearing away rubbish.

2. Special attendance on Nominated Sub-Contractors shall be given as an item in each case, giving particulars of the requirement such as unloading, storing, hoisting, placing in position, providing special scaffolding, weather protection and environmental control, power, or any other services not included under general attendance.

Section B
PRELIMINARIES

B.1 GENERAL RULES
1. For general rules see Section A.
2. The Tender enquiry documentation shall contain sufficient information to enable the Tenderer to ascertain the nature and extent of the Works together with the associated liabilites and responsibilities.
3. Items shall be given within the Preliminaries Section for the Tenderer to price requirements which shall include but not be limited to the particulars contained in the following Clauses.

B.2 PARTICULARS OF CONTRACT
1. Particulars of the form and type of Contract.
2. The names and addresses of the parties to the Contract.
3. Details of the form, duration and value of any Performance Bond required.
4. Requirements for any Parent Company Guarantee.

B.3 DESCRIPTION OF SITE
1. Where work is to be executed on a site or facility provided by the Employer, the location of the site or facility shall be stated together with any restrictions on access and arrangements for visiting the site or facility. A key plan, where available, shall be issued with the Tender Documents.
2. Details of any staged possession of the site.

B.4 DESCRIPTION OF FACILITY
Where work is to be executed within a facility provided by the Contractor this shall be stated together with details of any special construction facilities required for the completion of the work, such as minimum wharf length, total load-out weight and water depth.

B.5 DESCRIPTION OF WORKS
1. The Works shall be adequately described including details of work required to be executed or completed in a specific order or sections or phases.
2. Arrangements for the inspection of drawings, models and other information.

B.6 REQUIREMENTS, RESTRICTIONS AND OBLIGATIONS
1. Particulars of any Rules, Regulations, Standards, Specifications and the like with which the Works are to comply.
2. Special limitations on working operations, hours of work, access and the like.
3. Particulars of any obligation or restriction that may be imposed on the Contractor either in the way that work is to be carried out or on site personnel.
4. Details of direct contractors to be employed on the site during the period of the Contract advising of any co-ordination of programmes and any restrictions that may be imposed. Where not measured in accordance with Section C, attendances on direct contractors shall be described.
5. Where a site has been Nominated by the National Joint Council for the Engineering Construction Industry this shall be stated and a copy of the Supplementary Project Agreement, where available, shall accompany the Tender enquiry document.
6. Details of any Local or Site Agreement other than covered in Clause B.6.5 hereof.

B.7 INSURANCES
Details of all provisions to be made for insurances.

B.8 CONTRACTOR'S ARRANGEMENTS
1. Particulars of Contractor's administrative arrangements which shall include requirements for the supervision and administration of the site.
2. Particulars of the method to be used for recording and monitoring progress.
3. Temporary site accommodation including sheds, offices, messrooms, sanitary accommodation and the like. Heating, lighting, furniture and equipment, rates and attendance shall be deemed to be included.
4. An item shall be given to allow the contractor to price any obligation that he feels attracts cost and which has not otherwise been specifically listed herein.

B.9 EMPLOYER'S REQUIREMENTS

Where not given in accordance with the requirements of Section C, particulars shall be given of any requirements of the Employer or the Employer's representatives including:

1. Vehicles
2. Attendance of staff such as drivers and laboratory assistants.
3. Equipment such as protective clothing, survey and laboratory equipment.
4. Special requirements for programme or progress charts.
5. Progress photographs.
6. Signboards.

B.10 LOCAL AUTHORITIES AND PUBLIC UNDERTAKINGS

Unless otherwise provided the following shall be given as Prime Cost or Provisional Sums.

1. All fees and charges which the Contractor is required to pay to Local Authorities.
2. Work which is to be carried out by a Local Authority or Public Undertaking.

B.11 OTHER REQUIREMENTS

Where required, items shall be given for the following procedures:

1. Financial reporting and cost control.
2. Method of evaluating the final account.
3. Progress payments and final settlement.
4. Daywork.
5. Variation price.
6. Quality Assurance.
7. Materials and stores control.
8. Removal of rubbish and maintenance of site facilities.
9. Cleaning the Works on handover or prior to commissioning.
10. Security.
11. Provision of record drawings, operating manuals or the like. (See also Clause A.4).

B.12 CONTINGENCIES

Provision for Contingencies shall be given as a Provisional Sum.

Section C
CONSTRUCTION SITE SERVICES

C.1 GENERAL RULES

For general rules see Section A.

C.2 GENERAL REQUIREMENTS

Items shall be given to cover the following temporary works and services:

1. Temporary works or services to be provided by the Contractor for the use of the Employer or Engineer. The description shall detail which, if any, of these items the Contractor will be allowed to use.
2. Scaffolding for the Works shall be given as an item, unless measured in accordance with Section D, or provided by others.
3. The construction of any dock and harbour facilities shall be described detailing cranage and berthing capacity.
4. Responsibility for maintenance, dismantling, storage and clearing away shall be stated within the description.
5. Any requirement to permit the use by other contractors of the Contractor's temporary works and services shall be given detailing maintenance and charging arrangements.
6. Construction site services not measured under this Section shall be deemed to be included, as provided in Clause A.7.9.
7. Details of temporary works and services provided by others for the use of the Contractor shall be given stating responsibility for maintenance and charging arrangements.

C.3 COMMISSIONING

1. Requirements for commissioning the Works, including the provisions of commissioning engineers, shall be described.
2. The temporary operation of any installation, except for testing, shall be given as an item stating the duration and purpose.
3. The provision of Contractor's personnel to work under the instructions of a Vendor shall be described stating the duration and the plant or equipment being commissioned.
4. The provision of consumables including feed stocks, fuels and temporary services, the provision of test blanks, drains, vents and the like, shall be described and shall include the subsequent removal of surplus or spent materials.

Section D
SCAFFOLDING

D.1 GENERAL RULES

For general rules see Section A

D.2 WORK INCLUDED

This Section applies in those instances where the nature and extent of scaffolding can be predetermined. The rules may also be applied to establish a list of items for a Schedule of Rates which will enable scaffolding to be measured and priced when the detailed requirements are known.

D.3 DEFINITIONS

The following definitions shall apply:

1. Putlog scaffold—single scaffold with one end of putlog fixed to permanent structure and other end to single line of standards and ledgers. Normally five boards wide with toe board and single guard rail along one side.
2. Independent scaffold—free standing scaffold with no internal standards and which is not a tower. Normally five boards wide with toe board and single guard rail.
3. Birdcage scaffold—free standing scaffold with a surface area on plan exceeding 9.00 m2. Close boarded with toe boards and single guard rail.
4. Independent Tower— similar to Birdcage scaffold but with a surface area on plan not exceeding 9.00 m2.
5. Mobile Tower—similar to Independant Tower but provided with wheels and ladders to give internal access to platform.
6. Cantilever or Built-Out scaffold—scaffold raked out from existing scaffold or structure containing one lift only. Five boards wide with toe board and single guard rail along one side. Any additional lifts to be measured under appropriate items.
7. Platform scaffold—scaffold erected on existing scaffold or structure containing one lift only. Close boarded with toe boards and guard rails.
8. Bridging scaffold—scaffold erected between existing scaffold and structure with each end supported. Spans of over 6.00m shall be described and given separately. Close boarded with toe boards and single guard rails along two exposed sides.
9. Ramp scaffold—similar to Bridging scaffold but with ends at differing levels.
10. Suspended Soffit scaffold—freely supported scaffold with ends supported by hangers. Close boarded including toe boards and single guard rails on all sides.
11. Decking—shall mean timber boards as required and shall be deemed to include toe boards and single guard rails.
12. Barriers—standards to be generally at 1.5m centres suitably secured.
13. Generally—the foregoing scaffold systems shall be deemed to include all necessary ladders, ledgers, transoms, bracing, ties, anchorages, clips, base plates and boards.
14. Maintenance—shall mean taking over responsibility of completed scaffolds from the erectors, and shall include registrations, regular inspections, upkeep for safety purposes, and all costs and hire charges until the authorised dismantling date.

D.4 PARTICULARS OF WORK

1. Scaffolding shall be described according to location as follows:
    - (a) Internal.
    - (b) External.
    - (c) Below datum, stating whether in trench, pipe track or the like.
    - (d) In vessels.
2. Scaffolding to curved structures shall be given separately.
3. Scaffolding to be used for load bearing or hoisting shall each be given separately.
4. Where scaffolding material is free issue this shall be stated.
5. Scaffolding shall be identified as follows:
    - (a) Supply (where applicable) and erection.
    - (b) Hire (where applicable) and maintenance of standing scaffolding stating period of requirement. Where the period of requirement of standing scaffolding cannot be specified a schedule of items for the periodic hire and/or maintenance shall be given.
    - (c) Dismantling and removal.

D.5 GROUPING

Scaffolding shall be grouped according to the material specification as follows:

1. Steel tube.
2. Galvanised tube.
3. Sheradised tube.
4. Alloy tube.
5. Special systems such as self lock scaffolding.

D.6 MEASUREMENT AND CLASSIFICATION

Unless otherwise stated, scaffolding and associated items shall be measured and classified as follows, giving the commencement level above datum in successive stages of 6.00m.

1. Putlog scaffold shall be given in metres stating the height of top decking above commencement level in successive stages of 2.00m and stating the method of attachment.
2. Independent scaffold shall be given as for Putlog scaffold.
3. Cantilever or Built—Out scaffold shall be given as for Putlog scaffold.
4. Birdcage scaffold shall be given in square metres measured on plan stating the height of top decking above commencement level in stages of 2.00m.
5. Independent Tower shall be given as for Birdcage scaffold.
6. Mobile Tower shall be given as for Birdcage scaffold.
7. Platform scaffold shall be given as for Birdcage scaffold.
8. Bridging scaffold shall be given as for Birdcage scaffold, stating the number.
9. Ramp scaffold shall be given in square metres measured on plan stating the average height of decking above commencement level in successive stages of 2.00m.
10. Suspended Soffit scaffold shall be given in square metres measured on plan stating distance of decking below commencement level in successive stages of 2.00m and stating the method of attachment.
11. Decking shall be given in square metres measured on plan and voids of circular and irregular shape less than 14.00 m2 shall not be deducted.
12. Barriers shall be given in metres stating the height and number of rails.
13. Protective panels and sheeting shall be given in square metres describing the material to be used and the method of attachment. Laps and joints shall be deemed to be included.
14. Temporary lighting standards shall be enumerated stating the height.

Section E
STEELWORK

E.1 GENERAL RULES
For general rules see Section A.

E.2 INFORMATION
1. A general description of the work in this Section shall be given where it is not evident from the location drawings required to be provided by this document.
2. The following information, where available, shall be shown on drawings which shall accompany the enquiry documents:
   - (a) The position of the work in relation to other parts of the work and of the proposed structures.
   - (b) The types and sizes of structural members and their positions in relation to each other.
   - (c) Details of connections or particulars of the reactions, moments and axial loads at connection points.
3. Where the Contractor is required to produce any or all of the foregoing information details of the requirements shall be given.

E.3 PARTICULARS OF WORK
1. Particulars of the following shall be given:
   - (a) Grade or grades of steel.
   - (b) Supply, whether by Contractor or free issue.
   - (c) Limits of tolerance.
   - (d) Methods of fabrication and the type of site connections.
   - (e) Tests of the materials stating the number required.
   - (f) Tests of workmanship to be carried out during fabrication stating the number required.
   - (g) Tests of the finished work stating the number required.
   - (h) Non-destructive testing shall be given separately.
2. Temporary steelwork provided by the Contractor for the Works shall not be included except in the case of any special temporary structural steelwork specifically requested.

E.4 GENERALLY
1. All items shall be given by weight unless otherwise stated.
2. The weight of mild steel shall be taken for the purposes of calculation to be 7.85 tonnes per cubic metre unless otherwise specified.
3. No allowance shall be made for rolling margin or the weight of weld metal.
4. All cutting, drilling, welding, bolting and the like shall be deemed to be included except where otherwise provided under Clause E.6.8.
5. No deduction in weight shall be made for splay cut ends, mitres, notches, holes, slots and the like.
6. Plates of irregular shape, including those used in the fabrication of structural members, shall be weighted based on the net area.

E.5 GROUPING
Steelwork in each different and independent structure, rack, bridge, module or skid shall be given separately under an appropriate heading and shall be sub-divided to distinguish between:
1. The supply and fabrication of steelwork.
2. The erection of steelwork.
3. The supply and fixing of miscellaneous metalwork.
4. Where the supply, fabrication and erection or the fabrication and erection of steelwork is required to be grouped together, this shall be so stated and measured as for supply and fabrication.

E.6 SUPPLY AND FABRICATION
1. The supply and fabrication of structural members shall be measured as the weight after fabrication subject to Clause E.4. Tubular sections shall be separately identified.
2. All caps, bases, haunches, cleats, gussets, stiffeners, curbings, brackets, rivets, bolts, nuts, shims, washers and the like shall be weighted in with the item to which they are attached in fabrication.
3. The supply and fabrication of steelwork shall be classified as follows:
   - (a) Grillages.
   - (b) Columns.
   - (c) Built-up columns.
   - (d) Beams.
   - (e) Deck framing.

E.6 SUPPLY AND FABRICATION (contd.)

        (f)   Built-up girders.
        (g)   Castellated sections.
        (h)   Tapered sections.
        (j)   Built-up box or hollow sections.
        (k)   Portal frames.
        (l)   Trusses.
        (m)   Trestles.
        (n)   Towers.
        (p)   Bracings.
        (q)   Purlins.
        (r)   Rails for overhead cranes.
        (s)   Cladding rails.
        (t)   Deck or side panels.
        (u)   Stairways and landings.
        (v)   Walkways and platforms.
        (w)   Ladders, stating whether caged.
        (x)   Padeyes or padears.
        (y)   Sea fastenings.

4. Curved, cambered or cranked members shall each be given separately.
5. Members comprising boom and infill construction shall be given separately.
6. The weight of steelwork members for the support of ductwork, pipework, electrical or instrumentation work which are attached to the structural frame during fabrication shall be added to the items to which they are attached. In all other cases reference shall be made to Sections G, H, J and K. Specific support structures including bridges, trestles and the like shall be given separately and measured in accordance with Clause E.6.
7. Anchorages and holding-down bolt assemblies shall be enumerated and described and shall include packings and wedges. Where these assemblies are to be handed to other contractors for fixing this shall be stated.
8. The welding of joints and connections:
    (a)   Where steelwork is described as welded, the welding of joints and connections in all positions shall be deemed to be included with the items on which they occur, together with all cutting, cleaning, bevelling, grinding, machining, pre-heating, tack welding, sealing runs at weld roots and temporary backstraps.
    (b)   Alternatively, the welding of joints and connections required in the fabrication of steelwork and in the asssembly of modules shall be described and given separately in metres. Welding so measured shall be deemed to include work to all profiles and to square, raking or curved members. Designation of plate thickness for butt welding rates shall be the thickness of plate or members in which the weld occurs, irrespective of the angle subtended by the adjoining welded member. Fillet welds shall be measured by the dimension of the weld leg. Sealing runs at the root of butt welds and joints required due to Contractors' construction methods shall be deemed to be included.

E.7 ERECTION

1. The erection of structural members shall be measured in accordance with Clause E.6.1 and classified as follows:
    (a)   Grillages, columns, beams, frames and the like, stating the number of items.
    (b)   Trusses, trestles, towers, bracings, stairways, platforms and the like, stating the number of items.
    (c)   Bridges.
    (d)   Modules. Separate items shall be given for sea fastenings.

2. All caps, bases, haunches, cleats, gussets, stiffeners, curbings, brackets, rivets, bolts, nuts, shims, washers and the like shall be weighted in with the item to which they are attached in fabrication.
3. Trial erections of structural members shall be described and given by weight.
4. Welded connections for cathodic protection shall be enumerated. Cabling shall be measured in accordance with Section J.

E.8 MISCELLANEOUS METALWORK

1. Item descriptions shall state the principle dimensions and thickness and shall be deemed to include fabrication unless otherwise described. Items shall include all metal components and attached pieces. No deduction shall be made for openings or holes less than 0.50 m2 in area.
2. The supply and fixing of miscellaneous metalwork shall be measured and classified as follows:
    (a)   Pressed metal purlins, rails and accessories shall be given by weight.
    (b)   Gutters and downpipes shall be given in metres and shall be deemed to include all fittings.
    (c)   Permanent shuttering shall be given in square metres stating whether temporary supports are required.
    (d)   Wall cladding and roof decking shall be given in square metres; filler pieces, flashing pieces, upstands and the like shall be given in metres.
    (e)   Handrails and intermediate rails shall each be given in metres with posts and other supports each being enumerated.
    (f)   Bridge parapets shall be given in metres, measured along their top members.

E.8 MISCELLANEOUS METALWORK (contd.)

    (g)   Rectangular frames shall be given in metres, measured along the perimeter.

    (h)   Fenders shall be given in metres, measured along the perimeter.

    (j)   Duct covers, complete with frames, shall be given in metres.

    (k)   Floor plates and gratings including those to landings and platforms shall be given in square metres, stating whether plain, chequered or open mesh. Treads shall be enumerated.

    (l)   Tie rods shall be enumerated.

    (m) Walings shall be enumerated.

    (n)   Bridge bearings shall be enumerated, stating the type.

E.9 SURFACE TREATMENTS

    1.   Off site preparation and treatment shall be included with the item on which it occurs. The type of preparation and treatment shall be described stating whether before or after fabrication.

    2.   Surface treatment carried out on site after erection, shall be measured as a Protective Covering under Section M.

Section F
PLANT

F.1 GENERAL RULES
For general rules see Section A.

F.2 WORK INCLUDED
This Section applies to all major items of permanent plant, equipment, machinery, columns, towers, vessels, tanks or spheres together with their ancillary items and inter-connecting steelwork. The supply and connection of services together with permanent protective coverings and thermal insulation shall be measured within the appropriate sections.

F.3 PARTICULARS OF WORK
1. The description of each item shall include the approximate overall size and weight, plant item reference number where applicable, type of material, and approximate elevation in relation to datum.
2. The description of tanks and spheres shall, in addition, include volume, number of strakes, area of roof and the number of legs as applicable.
3. Where the Contractor is required to supply the item a full specification shall be provided including details of capacities, pressures, performance data, surface finish and the like.
4. Where items are to be supplied as free issue to the Contractor this shall be stated, listing the component parts where the item is to be assembled by the Contractor and detailing where the item is to be collected or received.
5. Any special requirements or other essential particulars shall be described including:
   - (a) Work which is to be carried out under the direction of a plant, equipment or machinery manufacturer or supplier.
   - (b) Attendance on work to be carried out by a plant, equipment or machinery manufacturer or supplier detailing facilities to be provided.
   - (c) Responsibility for and restrictions affecting lifting arrangements or attachments together with arrangements for the provision and removal of hardstandings and lifting aids.
   - (d) Testing including details of responsibility for the provision of attendant labour, materials and equipment.

F.4 GROUPING
The work shall be classified according to either:
1. Its location by area classification, eg. on plot, off plot, utilities area.
2. The system or process of which it forms part.

F.5 MEASUREMENT
All items of plant, equipment, machinery, columns, towers, vessels, tanks and spheres shall be enumerated and shall be deemed to include any necessary assembly, orientation, alignment, levelling and bolting down together with the provision of shims and packing pieces, the clocking of couplings between drivers and rotating equipment and trial running.

F.6 ANCILLARY ITEMS
1. Traying for vessels shall be given in square metres or enumerated stating:
   - (a) Type of tray.
   - (b) Number of pieces and method of fixing each level of tray including down-comers.
   - (c) Number of trays per vessel.

2. Charging columns, towers and the like shall be given by weight or volume stating:
   - (a) Type of material.
   - (b) Method of charging, including the provision and placement of any packing rings.
3. Welding shall be given in metres stating the item of plant, equipment or machinery to which it relates, the type of weld, the thickness of metal to be welded and details of requirements for preheating, stress relieving and non-destructive testing.
4. Where the Contractor is required to supply a template to a third party showing holding down bolt locations, this shall be enumerated.
5. Anti-vibration mountings shall be enumerated stating the size.

F.7 PRESERVATIVE AND PREVENTATIVE MAINTENANCE
Preservative and preventative maintenance shall be described and given as an item.

Section G
DUCTWORK

G.1 GENERAL RULES
For general rules see Section A.

G.2 WORK INCLUDED
This Section applies to all types of ducted installations.

G.3 GROUPING
1. Ductwork shall be grouped under the following headings:
   - (a) Ductwork fabrications.
   - (b) Ductwork erection.
   - (c) Equipment.
   - (d) Control gear.
   - (e) Supporting steelwork.
   - (f) Testing.
   - (g) Sundries.
2. The foregoing shall be further subdivided to distinguish between:
   - (a) Material or equipment supplied as free issue to the Contractor.
   - (b) Material or equipment of the Contractor's own supply.
   - (c) Material or equipment obtained from a nominated supplier or fabricator.
3. Where fabrication and erection of ductwork is required to be grouped together this shall be so stated and measured as for fabrication.

G.4 PARTICULARS OF WORK
1. Any special requirements or other essential particulars shall be stated, for example:
   - (a) The extent of protection before and after installation or fabrication, including requirements for touching up and making good.
   - (b) The extent and method of any internal cleaning required.
   - (c) Fabrication specifically required on site or off site.
   - (d) Work which will be carried out under the direction of an equipment manufacturer or supplier.
2. Ductwork and associated fittings shall be classified according to size or weight as appropriate and given separately by specification and material.
3. Ductwork wall thickness shall be given in millimetres, or when appropriate in inches or by gauge.
4. The description of each item of equipment shall include approximate overall size, approximate total weight, plant item reference number where applicable, type of material and approximate elevation in relation to datum.
5. Where the Contractor is required to supply plant, equipment or machinery a full specification shall be provided including details of capacities, pressures, performance data and the like.
6. Where equipment is to be supplied for assembly by the Contractor a description of component parts shall be given and details of where the item is to be collected or received.

G.5 MEASUREMENT
1. Ductwork shall be measured along the centre line excluding items of in-line equipment such as valves and flow meters but through all in-line fittings such as bends, branches, elbows, reducers and tees, the fabrication of which shall be enumerated and deemed to be Extra Over.
2. The fabrication or making of joints or connections and the provision and installation of earth continuity components shall be deemed to be included.

G.6 DUCTWORK FABRICATION
Measurement of items in each classification shall be grouped according to size under the following descriptions:
1. Ductwork shall be given in metres and shall include for the provision of straps, hangers and the like.
2. Any closing length for fabricated ductwork indicated on the drawing shall be added to the measurement.
3. In-line fittings shall be enumerated, each type of fitting being kept separate.
4. Access doors shall be enumerated stating the size and shall include forming the perforation in the duct wall.
5. Stop ends shall be enumerated.

G.6 DUCTWORK FABRICATION (contd.)

6. Air turning vanes, splitters and the like shall be enumerated, each type being kept separate. Alternatively such items may be included with the fitting to which they apply.
7. Plenums shall be enumerated.
8. Nozzles shall be enumerated, stating whether fixed or adjustable.
9. Flexible connections shall be enumerated and the length stated.
10. Forming test holes shall be enumerated.

G.7 DUCTWORK ERECTION

Measurement of items in each classification shall be grouped according to size under the following descriptions:
1. Ductwork shall be given in metres and shall include for the erection of all in-line fittings and for the erection of straps, hangers and the like.
2. Preparing ends of ductwork specifically required to be supplied over-length shall be enumerated and shall be deemed to include taking dimensions, templates, offering up and the like.
3. Installing access doors where not supplied already fixed in the duct length shall be enumerated.
4. Installing stop ends shall be enumerated.
5. Installing air turning vanes, splitters and the like, where not supplied as part of the fitting to which they apply, shall be enumerated.
6. Installing plenums shall be enumerated.
7. Installing nozzles shall be enumerated, stating whether fixed or adjustable.
8. Installing flexible connections shall be enumerated and the length stated.

G.8 EQUIPMENT

All items of equipment shall be enumerated and shall be deemed to include orientation, alignment, levelling and bolting down together with the provision of shims and packing pieces, the clocking of couplings between drivers and rotating equipment and trial running.

G.9 CONTROL GEAR

Control gear shall be enumerated and classified as follows:
1. Control valves and the like which shall be further classified according to type and size.
2. Electrical control gear shall be further classified according to type and size.

G.10 SUPPORTING STEELWORK

1. This Section applies to the supply, fabrication and erection of supporting steelwork required for the support of straps, hangers and the like:
    (a) Descriptions shall include the method of fixing to the parent structure and details of any finishing treatment required including galvanising, shot blasting, painting and the like.
    (b) The weight of supports, brackets and the like required to be given in accordance with the following clauses shall include all additional support necessary from the parent structure up to but not including the straps or hangers, except as otherwise noted hereafter.
    (c) No deduction in weight shall be made for splay cut ends, notches, holes, slots and the like. No addition in weight shall be made for rolling margin, bolts, nuts, washers, rivets or weld metal.
    (d) All cutting, drilling, welding, bolting and the like shall be deemed to be included.
    (e) Where appropriate, reference to any standard or detail drawing shall be given in the description.
2. Supports, brackets and the like fabricated from general steel sections shall be enumerated and classified in the following weight groups:
    (a) Not exceeding 5 kg.
    (b) Exceeding 5 kg but not exceeding 15 kg.
    (c) Exceeding 15 kg but not exceeding 25 kg.
    (d) Exceeding 25 kg but not exceeding 50 kg.
    (e) Exceeding 50 kg stating the total weight.

G.11 TESTING

Testing of ductwork and equipment shall be described and given as an item.

G.12 SUNDRIES

Wall sleeves, packings and the like shall be enumerated stating size and method of fixing where appropriate.

Section H
PIPEWORK

H.1 GENERAL RULES
For general rules see Section A.

H.2 WORK INCLUDED
This Section applies to all types of pipework whether fabricated on site or off site.

H.3 GROUPING
1. Pipework shall be grouped under the following headings:
    (a) General Pipework.
    (b) Jacketted Pipework.
    (c) Tracing – Carbon Steel and Copper.
    (d) Lined Pipework.
    (e) Other Pipework.
    (f) Coating and Wrapping.
    (g) Work to Existing.
    (h) Pipe Supports and Hangers.
    (j) Testing.
    (k) Ancillary Works.
2. The foregoing pipework shall be further sub-divided to distinguish between:
    (a) Pipework with materials supplied as free issue to the Contractor.
    (b) Pipework with materials of the Contractor's own supply.
    (c) Pipework with materials obtained from a Nominated Supplier or Fabricator.

H.4 PARTICULARS OF WORK
1. Any special requirements or other essential particulars shall be stated, for example:
    (a) The extent of protection before and after installation or fabrication, including requirements for touching up and making good.
    (b) The extent and method of any internal cleaning.
    (c) Fabrication specifically required on site or off site.
2. Pipework generally shall be classified according to nominal size and given separately by Specification and material.
3. Pipe wall thicknesses shall be in accordance with the given pipe schedule references, or, where appropriate, in millimetres or inches.
4. Where the Specification requires different types of welding these shall be given under separate headings.

H.5 MEASUREMENT
1. Pipework shall be measured along the centre line through all in-line fittings such as bends, elbows, branches, reducers and tees, the installation of which shall be enumerated and deemed to be Extra Over, but not through items of in-line equipment such as valves, flow meters and bellows units which shall each be measured separately. Where an in-line reduction in diameter occurs at a reducer or tee, the dominant diameter shall be measured over the full length of the fitting.
2. In the case of pipework for fabrication the closing length indicated on the drawings shall be added.
3. In the case of fabricated pipework spools the erection of pipework shall be deemed to include all bends, elbows, branches, reducers, tees, flanges, bosses, weldolets, sockolets, elbolets, thredolets, latrolets, nipples, plugs, couplings, unions, pipe caps and the like fixed to the fabricated pipe spool. Joints between spools or joints to equipment or in-line fittings shall be measured separately. Modifications to fabricated pipework for closing shall be measured with erection.
4. Field run pipework shall be measured in accordance with Clause H.5.1 or in the case of small bore pipework Clause H.5.8 and the erection shall be deemed to include any fabrication.
5. Pipework having flanged ends shall be measured from the face of the flange which is attached to the pipe being measured.
6. Flanged or welded joints shall be measured separately and, except where noted in the description, shall include for all necessary cutting to length, bevelling, cleaning of joint faces, tack welding, setting up and aligning.
7. Taper boring between pipes and/or fittings of varying schedules shall be enumerated stating the nominal sizes and schedules involved.
8. Pipework not exceeding 50 mm – 2'' nominal size, shall be measured along the centre line and shall include all joints, pulled bends, in-line fittings, fabrication and erection unless otherwise stated when measurement shall be in accordance with Clause H.5.1.

H.6 GENERAL PIPEWORK

Pipework under this heading shall include Carbon Steel, Low Alloy, Stainless Steel and High Alloy pipework, each being given under separate headings and measured as follows:

1. Fabrication and erection of pipework shall each be given in metres unless otherwise stated.
2. Square or oblique cutting including preparation to pipe where not included under the provisions of Clause H.5., shall each be enumerated.
3. Threading ends of pipe shall be enumerated.
4. Bends, elbows, reducers, tees, caps and the like fittings shall each be enumerated.
5. Flanges shall be enumerated. Weldneck, slip-on, socket welded and screwed flanges shall each be given separately stating the flange rating. The item shall be deemed to include the orientation of the flange.
6. Designed closure pieces shall be enumerated and shall include checking dimensions on site, making any necessary site sketches and templates and offering up spool or pipe for marking off.
7. Fabrication, erection and subsequent removal of temporary spools where specified shall be measured in accordance with the ruules for general pipework.
8. Blank flanges shall be enumerated stating the flange rating.
9. Spades or Spectacle blinds shall each be enumerated stating the rating.
10. Forming pulled bends shall be enumerated and shall be deemed to include any necessary cutting, preparation and setting up subsequent to bending and shall be grouped as follows:
    (a) Not exceeding 90 degrees.
    (b) Exceeding 90 degrees but not exceeding 180 degrees.
    (c) Exceeding 180 degrees but not exceeding 270 degrees.
    (d) Exceeding 270 degrees but not exceeding 360 degrees.
    The first bend on each piece of pipework shall be kept separate from subsequent bends. Pipework bent in a spiral shall be so described.
11. Forming pulled expansion loops, bends or elliptical bends shall be given in accordance with Clause H.6.10 and kept separate.
12. Making welded lobster-back bends shall be enumerated stating the number of segments.
13. Forming swaged or fabricated reducers shall be enumerated. The diameter of the ends shall be given stating whether the reduction is to be concentric or eccentric.
14. In-line equipment and the like shall each be enumerated. In the case of valves, the type of valve, the type of end and any necessary removal or repacking shall be stated. Equipment flange ratings shall be given where appropriate.
15. Butt, socket, fillet and sleeve welded joints shall each be enumerated.
16. Single mitred butt welded joints shall each be enumerated. Joints at different angles shall be grouped as follows:
    (a) Not exceeding 45 degrees.
    (b) Exceeding 45 degrees but not exceeding 90 degrees.
17. Bolted, flanged, screwed, sleeved or proprietary joints shall each be enumerated, stating where appropriate the flange rating and form of joint (gasket, ring, proprietary, bursting disc, insulating, etc.).
18. Flange orifice plates shall be enumerated stating the plate rating.
19. Cold drawn or pulled-up bolted flanged joints shall be enumerated.
20. Welded branch or stub-in connections shall be enumerated. Branches at different angles shall be grouped as follows:
    (a) Not exceeding 30 degrees stating the angle.
    (b) Exceeding 30 degrees but not exceeding 60 degrees.
    (c) Exceeding 60 degrees but less than 90 degrees.
    (d) 90 degrees.
21. Welded reinforced branch or stub-in connections shall be enumerated and shall be deemed to include the reinforcement. Branches at different angles shall be grouped in accordance with Clause H.6.20.
22. Welded dummy branch connections shall be enumerated and grouped as in Clauses H.6.20 and H.6.21.
23. Bosses, weldolets, sockolets, elbolets, thredolets, latrolets, nipples, plugs and the like shall each be enumerated, describing the method of jointing to the parent pipe.
24. Thermowells shall be enumerated. Socket welded, screwed and flanged thermowells shall each be given separately:
    (a) Socket welded thermowells shall be given by the outside diameter of the fitting and shall be deemed to include welding.
    (b) Screwed thermowells shall be given by the outside diameter of the fitting and shall be deemed to include tapping. Seal welding shall be described.
    (c) Flanged thermowells shall be given by the inside diameter of the wall tube and the flange rating shall be stated. The item shall be deemed to include closing the end of the well and welding.

H.7 JACKETED PIPEWORK

1. Jacketed pipework shall be measured in accordance with Clause H.6 except as specifically provided hereafter. The nature of the jacket and the nominal size of the parent and jacket tube shall be stated.
2. Jacketed pipework shall be given in metres and this shall be the length of the parent tube measured to the flanged or bevelled end.
3. Where a continuously welded jacket is to be fabricated and erected on site this shall be so described. The item shall be deemed to include longitudinal cutting of the jacket tube, preparation of edges and subsequent welding.

H.7 JACKETED PIPEWORK (contd.)

4. Compound items of work operations, including jacket terminations to either parent pipe or the jacket pipe-flange, spacers, special testing and the like shall each be enumerated and described.

H.8 TRACING — CARBON STEEL AND COPPER

1. Tracing pipework shall be given in metres in accordance with Clauses H.5 and H.6. In the case of multiple tracing each tracer shall be measured. Spiral or helical tracing shall be kept separate and so described stating the nominal size of the parent pipe and the number of complete turns per metre on that pipe.
2. Where tracing is fixed to a parent pipe the nominal size and method of jointing of the parent pipe shall be given detailing the method of fixing the tracing and stating whether in single or multiple tracing. Any other supports or hangers shall be measured in accordance with Clause H.13.
3. Pipework in manifold assemblies shall be measured in accordance with Clauses H.5 and H.6.
4. Steam traps, codensate pots, strainers and the like shall be measured as in-line equipment in accordance with Clause H.6.14.

H.9 LINED PIPEWORK

1. Lined pipework shall be measured in accordance with Clauses H.5 and H.6 except as specifically provided hereafter and shall be deemed to include all additional handling of pipe and fittings necessitated by virtue of the application or insertion of the lining material.
2. Lined pipework shall generally be grouped according to whether the lining is rigid or flexible, classified according to the nominal pipe size and given separately by Specification.
3. Flanged or sleeved joints shall be deemed to include all such additional work as is required by the Specification of the lining material used.
4. Pups or pipe extensions welded onto fittings shall be enumerated stating the length in stages of 100mm.

H.10 OTHER PIPEWORK

1. Other pipework shall comprise pipework of materials such as spun iron, reinforced glassfibre, GRP (Glass Reinforced Plastic), PVC/GRP, aluminium, cupro-nickel, plastic and rubber and shall be grouped by material Specification.
2. The pipework shall be measured in detail in accordance with Clauses H.5, H.6 and H.9 except as specifically provided for hereafter.
3. Spigot and socket joints shall be deemed to be included with the pipework item.
4. Welded joints, flanged joints and proprietary joints shall be deemed to include all such work as is required by the Specification of the piping material.

H.11 COATING AND WRAPPING

1. Wrapping of pipe shall be given in metres stating the nominal size, surface preparation and detailing whether the wrapping is to be applied at a specialist coating depot or on the site. The wrapping shall be measured over the full length of each pipe.
2. Making good wrapping of prewrapped pipework at made bends, stub-ins and the like shall be given in metres measured over the actual length of the repair.
3. The wrapping of pipe joints and other fittings on prewrapped pipework shall be enumerated.
4. Holiday detection or other testing to pipe coating shall be given as an item stating the type or types of testing required.

H.12 WORK TO EXISTING

The product carried by the pipework shall be stated.
1. Purging existing lines shall be given in metres stating purge material and nominal size of line.
2. Breaking flanged joints shall be enumerated stating the flange rating.
3. Hot or cold cutting or tapping to existing pipework shall each be enumerated.
4. Removing existing pipework shall be given in metres stating the nominal size of pipe and shall be deemed to include all fittings, attachments and materials in-situ including supports fixed to the pipework and removal to such location as specified. Pipework which is to be re-used shall be kept separate.
5. Removing existing flanged valve, flow meter, bellows unit or other in-line fitting shall each be enumerated and shall be deemed to include the breaking of joints and the removal to such location as shall be specified.
6. Removing insulation shall be given in metres stating the type and nominal size of pipe.

H.13 PIPE SUPPORTS AND HANGERS

1. Pipe supports, hangers and the like generally:

   (a) Descriptions shall include the method of fixing to the parent structure and details of any finishing treatment required, including galvanising, shot blasting, painting and the like.
   (b) The weight of supports, hangers and the like required to be given in accordance with the following Clauses shall include everything necessary from the point of support except as otherwise noted hereafter.
   (c) No deduction in weight shall be made for splay cut ends, notches, holes, slots and the like. No addition in weight shall be made for rolling margin, bolts, nuts, washers, rivets or weld metal.

H.13 PIPE SUPPORTS AND HANGERS (contd.)

      (d) All cutting, drilling, welding, bolting and the like shall be deemed to be included.

      (e) Where appropriate, reference to any standard or detail drawing shall be given in the description.

2. Supports, hangers and the like fabricated from general steel sections shall be enumerated and classified in the following weight groups:

      (a) Not exceeding 5 kg.

      (b) Exceeding 5 kg but not exceeding 15 kg.

      (c) Exceeding 15 kg but not exceeding 25 kg.

      (d) Exceeding 25 kg but not exceeding 50 kg.

      (e) Exceeding 50 kg stating the total weight.

3. Supports, hangers and the like fabricated from proprietary steel sections shall be enumerated and classified in accordance with Clause H.13.2.

4. Proprietary supports and fittings including constant and variable hangers, split sleeve guides, rollers and the like:

      (a) Shall each be enumerated. Where appropriate, the weight shall be given.

      (b) Any assembly of components shall be deemed to be included.

5. Holding down bolts, anchor bolts and the like:

      (a) Shall each be enumerated.

      (b) Grouting shall be given in the description.

H.14 TESTING

1. Non-destructive testing shall be enumerated and given under separate headings such as Gamma Ray, X-Ray, Ultrasonic, Dye Penetration and the like.

2. Magnetic Particle Inspection shall be given as an item.

3. Testing pipework shall be given as follows:

      (a) Testing items shall be deemed to include all necessary cutting, jointing and the like, temporary removal and replacement of in-line equuipment and instruments, blanking off ends and temporary works associated with testing, provision of equipment and completion of test records. The responsibility for the supply of replacement gaskets, bolts and the like shall be stated.

      (b) The location at which testing is to be carried out shall be given under appropriate headings:

         (i) In Fabrication Shop stating whether on site or off site.

         (ii) On site in final position, including sectional testing.

      (c) The responsibility for the provision of water or air shall be stated together with details of any charges, storage provisions, drain off, disposal and the like.

      (d) Testing of fabricated spool pieces shall be enumerated stating the nominal size of the dominant pipe.

      (e) Line testing of pipework shall be given in metres measured overall stating the nominal size of the dominant pipe. The length shall be measured on the centre line through all in-line fittings and equipment such as valves, flow meters, exchanges and other main plant items.

H.15 ANCILLARY WORKS

1. Stress relieving completed welds shall be enumerated and described stating the material, wall thickness and nominal size of pipe.

2. Stress relieving completed fabrications shall be given either:

      (a) By weight or,

      (b) By furnace load and enumerated.

3. Pipeline identification shall be enumerated as follows stating the materials to be used:

      (a) Weld tags.

      (b) Valve or Equipment tags.

      For banded colour coding and flow indicators see Clause M.6.7.

4. Pickling of pipework shall be given as an item stating the chemical process, nominal size and lengths of pipework to be treated.

Section J
ELECTRICAL

J.1 GENERAL RULES

For general rules see Section A.

J.2 COMPOSITE UNITS

Particulars shall be given of the component parts of composite units together with details of any materials to be provided for assembly. Assembling and jointing shall be deemed to be included with the items.

J.3 PARTICULARS OF WORK

Descriptions shall include particulars of the following:
1. Material.
2. Supply, whether by Contractor or free issue.
3. Method of fixing.
4. Provision of fixing materials.
5. Nature of background.

J.4 GROUPING

Work shall be given under an appropriate heading and grouped as follows:
1. Conduit, trunking and the like.
2. Cables and conductors.
3. Accessories and fittings.
4. Switchgear, distribution gear and equipment.
5. Earthing tapes and fittings.
6. Supporting steelwork.
7. Sundries.

J.5 CONDUIT, TRUNKING AND THE LIKE

1. Conduit
   (a) Conduit shall be given in metres measured over all conduit fittings and conduit boxes stating the external size and method of jointing.
   (b) Bending, cutting, threading, jointing and all conduit fixings and fittings such as boxes, tees, bends, bushes, locknuts, and stopping plugs shall be deemed to be included.
   (c) Conduit descriptions shall include particulars of location including surface fixed, run in chase, embedded in screed, embedded in concrete and the like.
   (d) Boxes to receive accessories and fittings shall be given in accordance with Clause J.7.1.
   (e) Flexible conduits shall be enumerated stating the length and internal size. The type and number of terminations shall be given.
   (f) Forming openings for conduit entries in trunking, accessories, fittings, switchgear, distribution gear and equipment, providing associated components including bushes, locknuts, nipples and the like shall be deemed to be included with the items in which they occur.

2. Trunking
   (a) Trunking shall be given in metres measured on the centre line over all fittings stating the size of the trunking, the number and size of any compartments, the type of covers and the method of jointing.
   (b) Cutting and jointing trunking shall be deemed to be included.
   (c) Stop ends, bends, tees, crosses, offsets, reducers, internal fire barriers and the like shall be enumerated as Extra Over the trunking.

3. Trays
   (a) Trays and similar continuous supports shall be given in metres measured on the centre line over all fittings stating the size and method of jointing.
   (b) Cutting and jointing tray shall be deemed to be included.
   (c) Stop ends, bends, tees, crosses, offsets, reducers and the like shall be enumerated as Extra Over the tray.
   (d) Cutting openings in tray shall be enumerated and grouped together irrespective of size.

4. Ladder Rack
   (a) Ladder rack and similar supports shall be given in metres measured on the centre line over all fittings stating the size and the spacing of rungs.

J.5 CONDUIT, TRUNKING AND THE LIKE (contd.)

      (b)   Cutting and jointing ladder rack shall be deemed to be included.

      (c)   Elbows, risers, tees, crosses, reducers and the like shall be enumerated as Extra Over the ladder rack.

  5.   Sundries

      (a)   Earth continuity components shall be deemed to be included with the items.

      (b)   Supporting steelwork shall be given in accordance with Clause J.10.

      (c)   Treatments of cut edges of finished components shall be deemed to be included.

J.6 CABLES AND CONDUCTORS

  1.   Cables

      (a)   Cables shall be given in metres measured from gland to gland stating the size, number and size of cores and rating.

      (b)   The following standard allowances shall be added to cable measurement lengths for tails.
Switches, socket outlets, light fittings, equipment outlets and the like: 0.30 m.
All other items: 1.00 m.

      (c)   Cables which are required to be snaked or looped shall be so described.

      (d)   Cables laced and banded together in circuit groups, in trefoil or other formation shall be so described. Any banding or similar treatment shall be given in the description. Work in panels shall be given separately.

      (e)   Determining circuits, capping ends of cables (including end on drum or coil after cutting) providing draw wires and draw cables, cleaning out conduits, pipe ducts, trunking and trays, threading cables through sleeves and the like shall all be deemed to be included.

      (f)   Cables drawn into existing pipe ducts, conduits or trunking shall each be so described. Removing and replacing covers, inspection lids and the like, shall be given in the description.

      (g)   Dressing cables after installation shall be deemed to be included.

  2.   Locations

Cable descriptions shall include particulars of final location classified as follows:

      (a)   In trench or open duct.

      (b)   On arm or hanger.

      (c)   To cable tray, ladder rack or other surfaces.

      (d)   In underground pipe duct.

      (e)   In conduits or in trunking.

      (f)   Suspended from insulators or catenaries.

      (g)   Wrapped around pipework or equipment.

  3.   Cable Joints

      (a)   Cable termination joints, branch joints, line taps, through joints and joints to existing cables shall each be enumerated separately and the description shall include all jointing items such as end boxes, glands, seals, joint boxes, earth tags, identification ferrules and the like other than where included with items of switchgear or similar items.

      (b)   Removing cable insulation, sheaths and armouring, removing and replacing terminal covers, connecting conductors and providing heat, insulating material, jointing material, lock-nuts, bushes, cable connecting lugs, cable and core identification markers and the like, shall be deemed to be included.

      (c)   Forming openings for cable entries in trunking, accessories, fittings and the like, together with any bushing material, shall be deemed to be included.

      (d)   Forming openings for cable entries in switchgear, distribution gear and equipment after delivery shall be enumerated stating the size and the thickness of the material.

  4.   Cable Fixings

      (a)   Cable fixings including saddles, cleats, clips, hangers and the like shall be given in the description of the cables stating the nature of the background to which fixed. Alternatively, hangers and suspenders may be enumerated separately.

      (b)   D-irons, insulators and the like shall each be enumerated.

      (c)   Pylons and similar cable supports shall be given in accordance with Clause J.11.

J.7 ACCESSORIES AND FITTINGS

  1.   Accessories including switches, socket outlets, thermostats, bell pushes, signal indicating units, stop/start pushbuttons and the like shall each be enumerated stating the rating. Where accessories are in gangs the number in the gang shall be stated. All associated items such as boxes and earthing tails shall be given in the description.

  2.   Fittings

      (a)   Luminaires shall each be described and enumerated. Descriptions shall include associated items, such as boxes, connector blocks, cable and conduit pendants stating the length of suspension, earthing tails, reflectors, shades, lampholders, lamps and the like.

      (b)   Auxiliary fittings including clocks, telephones, alarm bells, loudspeakers and the like shall each be described and enumerated. All associated items such as boxes and cover plates shall be given in the description.

J.8 SWITCHGEAR, DISTRIBUTION GEAR AND EQUIPMENT

1. Generally
   - (a) Switchgear, distribution gear and equipment including prefabricated switchboards, isolator switches, switch fuses, distribution boards, starters, busbar chambers, motors, fans, batteries, rectifiers, feeder pillars, meters and the like shall each be enumerated stating the rated capacity and size. Forming openings in trunking together with any bushing material shall be deemed to be included. Openings formed prior to delivery and pre-drilled gland plates shall be given in the description.
   - (b) Composite units shall each be enumerated. Particulars of component parts shall be given together with details of any materials required for assembly. Assembling and jointing shall be deemed to be included.
   - (c) Transformers shall be enumerated stating the type, rating, size, weight and the method of fixing. Filled transformers shall be given separately stating the filling requirements.

2. Links, Fuses and the like.
   Links, fuses, miniature circuit breakers, gland plates, terminal boxes and the like which form part of the item shall be given in the item description.

J.9 EARTHING TAPES AND FITTINGS

1. Tapes
   - (a) Tapes shall be given in metres measured over all fittings.
   - (b) Bends, twists, termination joints, branch joints and through joints together with all jointing materials, drilling, sweating and tinning shall be deemed to be included.

2. Lightning Conductor and Earthing Equipment
   Lightning conductor and earthing equipment including air terminals, test clamps, earth plates, earth rods (including driving) and the like shall each be enumerated stating the type and size.

J.10 SUPPORTING STEELWORK

1. Supporting steelwork, generally
   - (a) Descriptions shall include the method of fixing to the parent structure and details of any finishing treatment required including galvanising, shot blasting, painting and the like.
   - (b) The weight of supports, brackets and the like required to be given in accordance with the following clauses shall include everything necessary from the point of support except as noted hereafter.
   - (c) No deduction in weight shall be made for splay cut ends, notches, holes, slots and the like. No addition in weight shall be made for rolling margin, bolts, nuts, washers, rivets or weld metal.
   - (d) All cutting, drilling, welding, bolting and the like shall be deemed to be included.
   - (e) Where appropriate, reference to any standard or detail drawing shall be given in the description.

2. Supports, brackets and the like fabricated from general steel sections, shall be enumerated and classified in the following weight groups:
   - (a) Not exceeding 5kg.
   - (b) Exceeding 5kg but not exceeding 15kg.
   - (c) Exceeding 15kg but not exceeding 25kg.
   - (d) Exceeding 25kg but not exceeding 50kg.
   - (e) Exceeding 50kg, stating the total weight.

3. Supports, brackets and the like fabricated and assembled from proprietary steel sections shall be enumerated and classified in accordance with Clause J.10.2.

4. Proprietary supports and fittings including constant and variable hangers, split sleeve guides, rollers and the like:
   - (a) Shall each be enumerated. Where appropriate, the weight shall be given.
   - (b) Any assembly of components shall be deemed to be included.

5. Holding down bolts, anchor bolts and the like:
   - (a) Shall each be enumerated.
   - (b) Grouting shall be given in the description.

J.11 SUNDRIES

1. Pylons, poles and the like.
   - (a) Pylons, poles and the like together with their supporting brackets shall each be enumerated stating the size, method of fixing and the nature of the structure.
   - (b) Lamp standards shall be enumerated stating the size and method of fixing.
   - (c) Boring or excavating holes for poles and stays shall be deemed to be included.
   - (d) Catenaries shall be enumerated stating the type and the size. Eye-bolts, shackles and straining screws shall be given in the description stating the method of fixing.

2. Cable Trenches
   - (a) Sand for bedding cables in trenches, preformed ducts and draw pits shall be given in cubic metres stating the depth of sand and whether laid in one or more layers under and over cables. Disposal of any displaced excavated material shall be deemed to be included.
   - (b) Cable tiles, marker tapes and the like shall be given in metres stating the type and size.
   - (c) Route markers shall be enumerated. Any concrete surrounds shall be given in the description. Excavating shall be deemed to be included.

J.11 SUNDRIES (contd.)

3. Marking Holes.

    Marking out the position of holes, mortices, chases and the like to be cut or formed by others shall be given as an item.

4. Discs and Labels

    (a) Discs and labels for the identification of fittings and equipment shall be enumerated. Alternatively discs and labels may be given in the description of the items to which they refer.

    (b) Repeated markings on cables shall be given in the description of the cable stating the spacing.

5. Equipment

    Equipment ancilliaries to be handed to employer including loose keys, ancillaries, tools, spares, warning notices, shock treatment cards and the like shall be given in the description of the item to which they refer.

6. Testing and Commissioning

    (a) Inspecting and testing and the provision of associated reports and certificates shall be given as an item. Providing test equipment shall be deemed to be included.

    (b) Commissioning of the completed installation shall be given in accordance with Clause C.3.

7. Operating Installation

    Operating part or whole of the completed installation for purposes other than inspecting, testing or commissioning, shall be given as an item, stating the purpose, duration in hours and any additional insurance requirements. Providing and/or payment for electrical power shall be given as a Provisional or Prime Cost Sum.

Section K
INSTRUMENTATION

K.1 GENERAL RULES
For general rules see Section A.

K.2 GENERAL INFORMATION
1. The instrument and control system shall be described, indicating where appropriate the method of operation eg. pneumatic, hydraulic or electronic and whether local, remote or centralised.
2. The demarcation line between the instrumentation and the electrical and pipework sections shall be clearly stated.

K.3 PARTICULARS OF WORK
Descriptions shall include particulars of the following:
1. Material.
2. Supply, whether by Contractor or free issue.
3. Method of fixing.
4. Provision of fixing materials.
5. Nature of background.

K.4 GROUPING
Work shall be given under an appropriate heading and grouped as follows:
1. Conduit trunking and the like.
2. Cables and conductors.
3. Instrument pipework.
4. Instrument multicore tube assemblies.
5. Instrument equipment and the like.
6. Supporting steelwork.
7. Sundries.

K.5 CONDUITS, TRUNKING AND THE LIKE
Conduit, trunking, trays and ladder rack shall each be measured in accordance with Section J.5.

K.6 CABLES AND CONDUCTORS
Cables, cable joints, cable fixings and the like shall be measured in accordance with Section J.6.

K.7 INSTRUMENT PIPEWORK
1. Grouping.
   Instrument pipework shall be grouped according to specification or function such as follows:
   (a) Process connections.
   (b) Instrument air supplies.
   (c) Pneumatic signals.
2. Locations
   Instrument pipework descriptions shall include particulars of final location as follows:
   (a) On arm or hanger.
   (b) To cable tray, ladder rack or other surfaces.
   (c) In conduits or in trunking.
   (d) Wrapped around pipework.
3. Measurement
   (a) Pipework shall be given in metres measured along the centre line, stating the nominal size and shall include all joints, pulled bends, in line-fittings, fabrication and erection in accordance with Clause H.5.8, unless otherwise stated.
   (b) In-line equipment including valves and the like shall each be enumerated.
   (c) Complete assemblies including valve stations and the like shall each be enumerated.
   (d) For supporting steelwork See Clause K.10.
   (e) Any pickling, degreasing or other special cleaning requirements shall be given as separate items in accordance with Clause H.15.4.
   (f) Testing instrument pipework shall be given as an item stating the length of pipe and number of loops, according to application, type and material of pipework. Test media, test pressures and any special test requirements shall be stated. All necessary temporary work and connections, drains, vents, plugs, spades and blanks shall be deemed to be included.

K.8 INSTRUMENT MULTICORE TUBE ASSEMBLIES

1. Location
The description of instrument multicore tube assemblies shall include particulars of final location as follows:
- (a) On arm or hanger.
- (b) To cable tray, ladder rack or other surfaces.
- (c) In conduits or in trunking.

2. Measurement
- (a) Instrument multicore tube assemblies shall be given in metres measured from gland to gland, stating the type, number and size of cores. A standard allowance of 1.00m shall be added to the length for tails.
- (b) Tube assemblies which are required to be snaked or looped shall be so described.
- (c) Determining correct connections, capping ends of tube assemblies (including end on drum or coil after cutting), threading through sleeves and the like shall be deemed to be included.
- (d) Tube assemblies drawn into existing conduits, ducts or trunking shall each be so described. Removing and replacing covers, inspection lids, and the like shall be given in the description.

3. Joints
- (a) Termination joints of instrument multicore tube assemblies shall be enumerated stating the number and size of cores. The item shall include all jointing items, glands, lock-nuts, identification ferrules other than those included with instruments, junction boxes, etc, and the forming of openings or the removal of knockouts.
- (b) Removing sheaths and armouring, removing and replacing terminal covers, connecting cores and fitting lock-nuts, bushes and identification ferrules shall be deemed to be included with the jointing items.
- (c) Junction boxes for tube assemblies shall be enumerated separately stating the type, the number of tube assemblies and the number and size of cores.

4. Fixings
Fixings for tube assemblies including saddles, cleats, clips, hangers and the like shall be given in the description of the tube assemblies. Alternatively hangers and suspenders may be enumerated separately.

K.9 INSTRUMENT EQUIPMENT AND THE LIKE

1. Control Panels
- (a) Control panels, consoles and the like shall each be enumerated stating the size and the method of fixing. Pre-drilled gland plates shall be given in the description.
- (b) Composite units shall each be enumerated. Particulars of the component parts shall be given together with details of any materials required for assembly and inter-links including wiring, tubing and the like. Assembling and jointing shall be deemed to be included.
- (c) Associated electrical equipment including emergency instrument power supply units, transformers, rectifiers and the like shall each be enumerated, stating the rating and capacity.
- (d) Associated mechanical equipment shall be given in accordance with the requirements of Section F.
- (e) Instrument housings shall be enumerated and described.
- (f) Testing control panels and the like shall be given as an item stating the testing requirements.

2. Capillaries
Filled system capillaries shall be enumerated stating the nominal length, size and the method of supporting.

3. Instruments
- (a) Instruments shall be classified according to "flow", "level", "temperature", "pressure" and like groupings and be enumerated.
- (b) The calibration and checking of instruments before and after installation shall each be given as an item stating the type of instrument.

4. Ancillaries
Instrument ancillaries such as air-pressure reducing/filter sets and voltage stabilising units shall each be enumerated.

K.10 SUPPORTING STEELWORK
Supports, brackets and the like shall be measured in accordance with Section J.10.

K.11 SUNDRIES

1. Pylons, poles and the like
- (a) Pylons, poles and the like together with their supporting brackets shall each be enumerated stating the size, method of fixing and the nature of the structure.
- (b) Boring or excavating holes for poles and stays shall be deemed to be included.
- (c) Catenaries shall be enumerated stating the type and size. Eye-bolts, shackles and straining screws shall be given in the description stating the method of fixing.

2. Cable Trenches
- (a) Sand for bedding cables in trenches, preformed ducts and draw pits shall be given in cubic metres stating the depth of sand and whether laid in one or more layers under and over cables. Disposal of any displaced excavated material shall be deemed to included.

K.11 SUNDRIES (contd.)

      (b)   Cable tiles, marker tapes and the like shall be given in metres stating the type and size.

      (c)   Route markers shall be enumerated. Any concrete surrounds shall be given in the description. Excavation shall be deemed to be included.

3. Marking, Holes, etc

Marking out the position of holes, mortices, chases and the like to be cut or formed by others shall be given as an item.

4. Discs and Labels

      (a)   Discs and labels for the identification of instruments and instrument equipment shall be enumerated. Alternatively discs and labels may be included with the items to which they refer.

      (b)   Repeated markings on instrument cables, pipework and tube assemblies shall be given in the description of the item stating the spacing.

5. Work by others

Inspection and approval of associated work performed by others such as installation of in-line instruments and instrument equipment shall each be described and given as an item.

6. Testing and Commissioning

      (a)   Functional testing of instrument systems and checking of alarms, trips and interlocks shall be described and given separately as an item.

      (b)   The provision of instrument air where required for functional testing shall be given separately as an item.

      (c)   The provision of associated reports and certificates, including those of any test equipment being provided, shall be given as items.

      (d)   Commissioning of the completed installation shall be given in accordance with Clause C.3.

7. Operating Installation

Operating part or whole of the completed installation for purposes other than inspection, testing or commissioning shall be given as an item, stating the purpose, duration in hours and any additional insurance required. Providing electrical power and instrument air shall be given as Provisional or Prime Cost Sums.

Section L
INSULATION

L.1 GENERAL RULES
For general rules see Section A.

L.2 WORK INCLUDED
This Section applies to all types of insulation to pipework, ductwork, vessels, equipment, machinery and the like.

L.3 PARTICULARS OF WORK

Each classification of insulation shall be divided to distinguish between:
- (a) Insulation with materials supplied as free issue to the Contractor.
- (b) Insulation with materials of the Contractor's own supply.
- (c) Insulation with materials obtained from a Nominated Supplier or Fabricator.
2. Any Special requirements or other essential particulars should be stated such as:
- (a) Protection before and after insulation.
- (b) Cleaning, painting or wrapping to surfaces prior to application.
- (c) Fabrication specifically required off site.
3. The work under the foregoing groupings may be further sub-divided into sections for fabrication and erection.

L.4 GROUPING
The work shall be grouped as follows and given under appropriate headings stating the specification and surface finish:
1. Pipework.
2. Ductwork.
3. Vessels, equipment and machinery.
4. Filling to voids.

L.5 MEASUREMENT
1. Items within this Section shall, unless otherwise stated, be deemed to include:
- (a) Fixings and adhesives.
- (b) Forming laps, welts, cut outs, recesses and the like.
- (c) Pointing, sealing, trowelling smooth, chamfered and sealed edges and the like.
- (d) Working around supports, small drains, vents or similar obstructions.
2. No deductions for areas or voids not exceeding 1.00 m2 or 0.05 m3 respectively shall be made.
3. Insulation to pipework shall be measured as fixed, along the centre line through all in line fittings such as bends, elbows, reducers, branches, tees, flanges and joints but excluding items of in line equipment such as valves, flow meters, bellows units and the like.
4. Insulation to ductwork, vessels, equipment, machinery and the like shall be measured on the surface to be covered. Finishing to all openings shall be deemed to be included unless otherwise stated.

L.6 PIPEWORK
1. Insulation to pipework shall be given in metres stating the nominal size of the pipe.
2. Insulation to in-line fittings such as bends, elbows, flanged joints and blank flanges shall each be enumerated.
3. Insulation to long radius bends and elbows shall be enumerated separately. Long radius shall mean exceeding two and half times the diameter of the pipe to be insulated.

4. Insulation to reducers shall be enumerated stating the nominal size of the larger end.

5. Insulation to branches or tees shall be enumerated stating the nominal size of the parent pipe except in the following cases where in addition the nominal size of the branch shall also be stated.
- (a) In the case of non-metallic surface finish the nominal size of the branch is two-thirds or more the nominal size of the parent pipe.
- (b) In the case of metallic cladding finish the nominal size of the branch is half or more than the nominal size of the parent pipe.
6. Insulation to proprietary joints shall be enumerated stating the type of joint.
7. Insulation to expansion or contraction joints shall each be enumerated.
8. Welded, screwed, socketed or proprietary joints left uninsulated for testing shall each be enumerated. The subsequent fixing of insulation over these joints shall be deemed to be included with the item.
9. Removable covers, boxes and the like shall each be enumerated.

L.6 PIPEWORK (contd.)

10. Insulation to valves and items of in-line equipment shall each be enumerated stating the diameter and type of valve or size and type of equipment together with the method of jointing to pipework.

L.7 TRACED PIPEWORK

Insulation to traced pipework shall be given separately and measured in accordance with Clause L.6. The type of tracing shall be stated. In the case of steam tracing the diameter and number of tracers shall be given.

L.8 JACKETED PIPEWORK

1. Insulation to jacketed pipework shall be given separately and measured in accordance with Clause L.6.

2. Insulation to special items as measured under Clause H.7.4 shall be enumerated.

L.9 DUCTWORK

1. Insulation to circular ductwork shall be given in square metres irrespective of size, stating the method of jointing of the ductwork. Bends, tapers and the like shall be enumerated.
2. Insulation to rectangular ductwork shall be given in square metres stating the sectional size and the method of jointing of the ductwork. Bends, tapers and the like shall be enumerated.
3. Insulation to change section pieces between circular and rectangular ductwork shall be enumerated stating the ductwork sizes and change section piece lengths.
4. Insulation to access doors shall be enumerated as Extra Over stating the door size.

L.10 VESSELS, EQUIPMENT AND MACHINERY

1. Insulation to vessel, equipment or machinery surfaces shall either be detailed and enumerated or shall be given in square metres stating the following:—
   (a) Type of structure, such as flanged, riveted or lapped plate.
   (b) Method of support, attachment, reinforcement and anchorage.
   (c) The welding of studs, lugs, support rings and the like where applicable.
2. Insulation to curved, conical or spherical items shall be given in square metres stating the radius.
3. Surfaces not exceeding 6.00 m2 shall be given in square metres and kept separate.
4. Insulation to expansion or contraction joints shall each be given in metres.
5. Insulation around projections, support rings and the like shall be given in metres.
6. Insulation to manholes, pockets, blanked-off branches and the like shall be enumerated as Extra Over stating the relevant sizes.
7. Insulation to manhole covers, pipe collars and the like shall each be enumerated as Extra Over stating the relevant sizes.
8. Insulation to flanges and the like shall be enumerated as Extra Over stating the relevant diameter.
9. Removable covers, boxes and the like shall each be enumerated.

Alternatively, where drawings are available, the insulation to vessels, equipment or machinery may each be enumerated as a composite item.

L.11 FILLING VOIDS

Insulation in filling to voids shall be given in cubic metres.

Section M
PROTECTIVE COVERINGS

M.1 **GENERAL RULES**

For general rules see Section A.

M.2 **WORK INCLUDED**

1. This Section applies to painting, linings, fireproofing and other protective coverings. Factory treatment, including shot blasting, galvanising and painting before delivery shall be measured within the appropriate Sections.
2. For coating and wrapping pipework see Section H.
3. For insulation see Section L.

M.3 **PARTICULARS OF WORK**

1. Descriptions shall include particulars of the following:
    (a) Materials.
    (b) Thickness and/or number of applications.
    (c) Surface finish.
    (d) Nature of background.
    (e) Any background preparation.
    (f) Method of application.
2. Further particulars of the following shall be included, where appropriate:
    (a) Method of fixing to background.
    (b) Laps, jointing and pointing.
    (c) Preparation of pre-applied coating and background to receive on site coatings at points of site connections and the like.
    (d) Special requirements associated with method of application.
    (e) Tests required of materials or finished work.

M.4 **GROUPING**

1. Work shall be grouped according to specification under an appropriate heading.
    (a) Protective coverings with materials supplied as free issue to the Contractor.
    (b) Protective coverings with materials of the Contractor's own supply.
2. Within each group, work shall be classified under the following sub-headings:
    (a) Inside work which shall be deemed to include any work protected from the weather both in internal and external locations.
    (b) Outside work which shall be deemed to include all work exposed to the weather.

M.5 **MEASUREMENT**

1. Work shall be measured on the surface to be covered and in the following categories unless otherwise stated:
    (a) Work on surfaces over 300 mm girth shall be given in square metres.
    (b) Work on surfaces not exceeding 300 mm girth shall be given in metres measured along the mean length.
    (c) Work on isolated surfaces over 300 mm girth but not exceeding 1.00 m2 shall be enumerated irrespective of size.
2. Work to corrugated or other irregular surfaces shall be described stating the nature of the corrugation or irregularity. No allowance shall be made to the net area for additional material required by the corrugation or irregularity.
3. No deduction to superficial measurements shall be made for voids not exceeding 1.00 m2.
4. All labours including making good or cutting and fitting to abutments, boundaries, projections, forming angles, arrises, ends, masking, temporary battens and the like shall be deemed to be included.

M.6 **PAINTING, SPRAYED COVERINGS AND OTHER APPLIED TREATMENTS**

1. Generally
    (a) Work to previously primed or painted surfaces shall be so described.
    (b) Work to be carried out on members before erection shall be so described.
    (c) Work to horizontal, sloping or vertical surfaces, and to soffits shall be grouped together.
    (d) Painting in multi-colours and cutting in edges shall be deemed to be included.
    (e) Reinforcement and preformed arrises shall be described and included within the items to be reinforced.

2. Beams, Columns, Cladding Rails and the like.

    Work to beams, columns, cladding rails and the like together with any associated braces, supports or similar items shall be grouped together.

3. Pipes and Circular Ducts

    (a) Work to pipes exceeding 50 mm — 2in. nominal size and circular ducts shall be given in metres, measured along the centre line of the pipe or duct over all joints, fittings, valves, flanges, in-line equipment and the like stating the nominal size of the pipe or duct.

    (b) Work to valves, flanges, in line equipment and the like on pipes exceeding 50 mm — 2in. nominal size and circular ducts shall be enumerated as Extra Over the pipe or duct.

    (c) Work to pipes not exceeding 50 mm — 2in nominal size shall be grouped together and given in metres, measured along the centre line of the pipe over all joints, fittings, valves, in-line equipment and the like.

    (d) Work to valves, flanges, in-line equipment and the like on pipes not exceeding 50 mm — 2in. nominal size shall be deemed to be included.

    (e) Work to associated straps, holderbats and the like shall be deemed to be included.

4. Rectangular Ducts

    (a) Work to rectangular ducts shall be given in square metres measured over all joints, fittings, in-line equipment and the like. The method of jointing shall be given.

    (b) Work to joints, fittings, flanges, in-line equipment, stiffeners, straps and the like shall be deemed to be included.

    (c) Work to rectangular/circular change section pieces shall be enumerated stating the cross sectional dimensions.

5. Vessels, Plant and Equipment

    (a) Work to vessels, plant and equipment shall be grouped together and either given in square metres or described and enumerated stating the overall size.

    (b) Work to branch joints, access doors, brackets, rivets, bolts and similar projections shall be deemed to be included.

6. Other Surfaces

    Work to other general surfaces shall be grouped together.

7. Code Bands and Letters.

    (a) Code bands to pipes, circular ducts and fittings exceeding 50 mm — 2in. nominal size shall be enumerated stating the nominal size of the pipe/duct and fitting to be coded and method of application.

    (b) Code bands to pipes and fittings not exceeding 50 mm — 2in. nominal size shall be grouped together and enumerated stating the method of application.

    (c) Letters or numerals, direction indicators and the like shall be enumerated separately stating the style, height and method of application.

8. Special Protection

    Where special protection in excess of masking dials, instruments and the like is required, this shall be described and given as an item.

M.7 CAST, PRECAST, BLOCK, BOARD AND SHEET LININGS AND COVERINGS

1. Generally

    (a) Work to be carried out on members before erection shall be so described.

    (b) Work to curved, conical or spherical surfaces shall each be kept separate stating the radius or radii.

    (c) Work to horizontal, sloping or vertical surfaces and to soffits shall each be kept separate.

    (d) Work cast or cut and fitted solidly around beam and column sections and the like shall be so described.

    (e) Formwork for cast insitu coverings shall be given in the description of the coverings.

    (f) Moulds for precast coverings shall be deemed to be included.

    (g) Reinforced and preformed arrises shall be described and included within the items to be reinforced.

2. Beams, Columns, Cladding Rails and the like

    Work which is cast or cut and fitted solidly around beam, column and cladding rail sections and the like shall be given in metres stating the cross section of the member.

3. Pipes and Circular Ducts

    (a) Work to pipes exceeding 50 mm — 2in. nominal size and circular ducts shall be given in metres, measured along the centre line of the pipe or duct over all joints, fittings, valves, flanges, in line equipment and the like, stating the nominal size of the pipe or duct.

    (b) Work to valves, flanges, in line equipment and the like on pipes exceeding 50 mm — 2in. nominal size and circular ducts shall be enumerated as Extra Over the pipe or duct. Coverings to the flanged items shall be deemed to include the associated flanged joints.

    (c) Work to pipes not exceeding 50 mm — 2in. nominal size shall be grouped together and given in metres measured along the centre line of the pipe over all joints, fittings, valves, in-line equipment and the like.

    (d) Work to valves, flanges, in-line equipment and the like on pipes not exceeding 50 mm — 2in. nominal size shall be deemed to be included.

    (e) Work to associated straps, holderbats and the like shall be deemed to be included.

M.7 CAST, PRECAST, BLOCK AND SHEET LININGS AND COVERINGS (contd.)

4. Rectangular Ducts
    (a) Work to rectangular ducts shall be given in square metres measured over all joints, fittings, in-line equipment and the like. The method of jointing shall be gven.
    (b) Work in boxing out of flanges, in-line equipment and the like shall be enumerated as extra over the ducts on which they occur stating whether fixed or removable.
    (c) Work to joints, fittings, stiffeners, straps and the like shall be deemed to be included.
    (d) Work to rectangular/circular change section pieces shall be enumerated stating the cross sectional dimensions.

5. Vessels, Plant and Equipment
    (a) Work to vessels, plant and equipment shall be grouped together and either given in square metres or described and enumerated stating the overall size.
    (b) Work to branch joints, brackets, rivets, bolts and similar projections shall be deemed to be included.

6. Other Surfaces
    Work to other general surfaces shall be grouped together.

7. Channels
    (a) Channel blocks, channel bases and sides shall each be given in metres measured along the mean length stating the overall size.
    (b) Outlets, ends and angles shall each be enumerated as Extra Over the channel.

8. Sundries
    (a) Access doors shall be enumerated as Extra Over stating the door size.
    (b) Returned ends, reveals, head cappings and the like shall be given in metres.
    (c) Forming cavities shall be given in square metres. Ties and the like shall be included within the description stating the spacings. Any necessary formwork shall be deemed to be included.
    (d) Raking and curved cutting to precast, block, board and sheet linings and coverings shall be deemed to be included within enumerated items and shall be given in metres in the case of items measured superficially.

ACKNOWLEDGEMENTS

The Association of Consulting Engineers
The British Constructional Steelwork Association
The Electrical Contractors' Association
The Institute of Construction Management
The Institution of Chemical Engineers
The Institution of Civil Engineers
The Institution of Mechanical Engineers
The Institution of Plant Engineers
The Pipeline Industries Guild
Thermal Insulation Contractors Association
Amoco (U.K.)
A. Anderson & Son (Electrical Engineers)
Babcock Power
Babcock Woodall-Duckham
N. G. Bailey
Balfour Beatty
Balfour Beatty Construction (Scotland)
Beck & Pollitzer
R. Blackett Charlton
Borax Holdings
BP Petroleum Development
British Nuclear Fuels
John Brown Engineers and Constructors
Cadbury Schweppes
Cape Contracts
Capper Neill (Management Services)
Costain Process Engineering & Construction
Crown House Engineering
Davy McKee
Esso Petroleum
Fluor (Great Britain)
Foster Wheeler Energy
Humphreys & Glasgow
Imperial Chemical Industries
Kitsons Insulation Contractors
Laing Industrial Engineering and Construction
The Lummus Company
William McCrindle & Son
Matthew Hall Engineering
Morceau (Fire Protection)
Motherwell Bridge Constructors
Palmers Scaffolding
Press Construction
Shell U. K. Oil
W. H. Smith & Company Electrical Engineers
Snamprogetti
Taylor—Woodrow Management and Engineering
J. D. & S. Tighe
United Kingdom Atomic Energy Authority
United Kingdom Construction & Engineering
Watney Mann & Truman Brewers
Whessoe Heavy Engineering
E. D. Williams & Sons
George Wimpey M.E. & C.
Worley Engineering